AUSTIN MAHONE
STARTIN' SOMETHING
SPECTACULAR

Mary Boone

TRIUMPH
BOOKS

Copyright © 2013 by Triumph Books LLC

No part of this publication may be reproduced, stored in a retrieval system, or transmitted in any form by any means, electronic, mechanical, photocopying, or otherwise, without the prior written permission of the publisher, Triumph Books LLC, 814 North Franklin Street, Chicago, Illinois 60610.

This book is available in quantity at special discounts for your group or organization. For further information, contact:

Triumph Books LLC
814 North Franklin Street
Chicago, Illinois 60610
(312) 337-0747
www.triumphbooks.com

Printed in U.S.A.

ISBN: 978-1-60078-976-2

Content developed and packaged by Rockett Media, Inc.
Written by Mary Boone
Edited by Bob Baker
Design and page production by Patricia Frey
Cover design by Patricia Frey

Photographs courtesy of Getty Images unless otherwise noted.

This book is not authorized, approved or endorsed by Austin Mahone, Chase Records or any organization or entity associated with or affiliated with Austin Mahone. It is not an official publication.

AUSTIN MAHONE

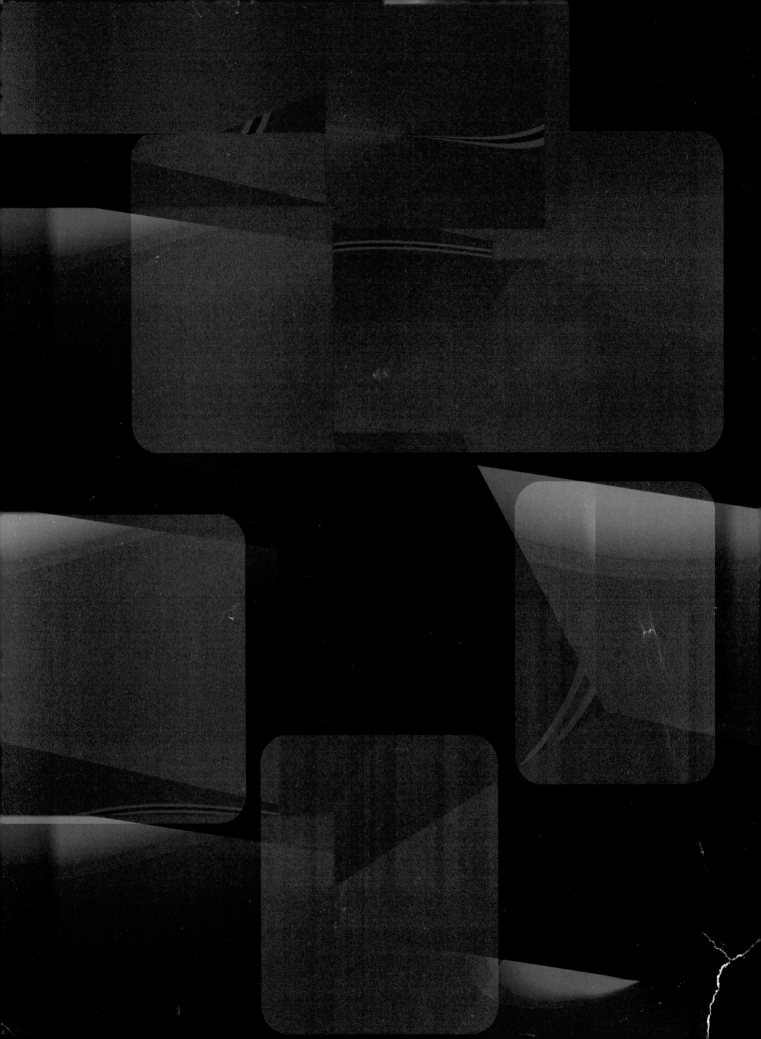

CHAPTER ONE

FROM TEXAS TO YOUTUBE AND BEYOND

He could have played a video game or read a book. Instead, Austin Mahone battled boredom by posting videos of himself online. He and his best friend, Alex Constancio, started posting videos in June 2010: silly skits, lip-synced music videos, ukulele-backed raps, even clips of them dancing to the hip-hop song "Teach Me How to Dougie."

"We started posting videos because we were bored," Austin told Just Jared in

"I promoted myself on Twitter and Facebook as hard as possible, nonstop," [Austin] told The Hollywood Reporter. "People started realizing that if they commented on my videos, I'd reply to their comment, so I started getting a lot more views and comments."

early 2013. "We had nothing better to do, so we started to do that as a hobby, and then it kind of just grew."

And grew and grew and grew.

Six months after posting his first videos, Austin began creating videos of himself singing covers of songs by artists including Justin Bieber, Adele, Bruno Mars and Drake. Thanks to social media, his legion of online fans swelled. His YouTube video covering Bieber's hit "Mistletoe" was posted in October 2011 and has since been viewed nearly 13 million times. In November 2011, even before landing a record deal, Austin debuted at No. 38 on Billboard's Social 50, a chart that combines Web presence and sales. He ranked higher than Demi Lovato, 50 Cent and Jennifer Lopez and just behind R&B diva Beyoncé.

Fast forward to spring 2013 – when Austin begins heading his own tour and joins Taylor Swift as the opening act on her RED tour – and it's clear that this Internet sensation has become a bona fide pop idol in less time than it takes some folks to spell S-U-P-E-R-S-T-A-R.

Austin Carter Mahone was born April 4, 1996, in San Antonio, Texas. His father, Carter Mahone, died when Austin was

Austin appears during Y100's Jingle Ball in Ft. Lauderdale, Fla., in December 2012. Photo courtesy of AP Images

just 16 months old. An only child, he and his mother, Michele Mahone, moved to the tiny town of La Vernia, Texas (population 1,055), when she remarried.

It was during his La Vernia years that Austin started posting his videos – first comedy, then music. He admits music hasn't always been his thing. Austin had a drum set and messed around with it for a while when he was 6 years old; it wasn't until YouTube commenters offered encouragement that he really began to get interested in music. His grandfather gave him a guitar and he started taking lessons. His singing, once limited to the shower, improved as it gained a worldwide following.

Uploading music videos is one thing, but Austin wanted to drive traffic to them.

"I promoted myself on Twitter and Facebook as hard as possible, nonstop," he told *The Hollywood Reporter*. "People started realizing that if they commented

Austin and his mom, Michelle, have a tight bond. Photo courtesy of *San Antonio Express-News*

Austin greets fans outside New York's Z100 radio station in June 2012. Photo courtesy of AP Images

Austin poses for photos with fans in Florida. Photo courtesy of AP Images

on my videos, I'd reply to their comment, so I started getting a lot more views and comments."

Gurj Bassi, digital director at Universal Music's Republic label, says the fact that Austin has taken the time to respond to fans has likely made a difference in his burgeoning career. "I always try to emphasize this to artists because fans love to have direct contact with the person they idolize, and the Internet makes that possible," said Bassi.

For Austin, that persistence and personal attention has paid off in a big way.

By January 2011, he had 2,000 YouTube fans; a month later, he had attracted 20,000 fans. In March 2011, he was invited to perform at a Playlist.com live concert in Orlando. By May 2013, his YouTube music channel had 802,000 subscribers and his 100-plus videos had attracted a combined 121 million views.

When his mom divorced her second husband, Austin moved back to San Antonio and briefly attended Lady Bird Johnson High School. He'd led a fairly ordinary life up to that point, but it was soon obvious he'd become famous enough that traditional school

Red Cheeked

Think celebrities don't trip, fall off chairs or spill food? Think again.

Austin told the folks at Scholastic's Stacks that his most embarrassing moment came when he was a little kid learning to water ski.

"Somehow my swim trunks like, just came off," he said. "I don't know how it happened. They didn't rip. Like my skis were on, so I don't know how it even happened."

"He wiped out and next thing you know, the skis are upside-down and he's in the water screaming, 'My swim trunks! My swim trunks!'" chimed in Austin's mom, Michelle Mahone. "So I thought for sure they just got torn off of him or something. He still had the skis on his feet, and the swim trunks were gone. We don't know how it happened. They were short skis, you know, because he was like 7 or 8 at the time. And then we saw them floating in the water and we went to get them. I thought they'd be torn, but they weren't. They were totally fine."

wasn't going to work any longer. Girls congregated at his locker, students began taking photos of him during class, and boys became resentful and started hassling him. Within five days, Austin and

MUSIC'S ALIVE IN SAN ANTONIO

Austin Mahone's hometown of San Antonio, Texas, is widely noted for its impressive live music scene and vibrant mix of subcultures.

The city plays host to a wide array of musical acts in small neighborhood bars, outdoor pavilions and entertainment complexes. In addition to the Alamodome, the major concert venues in town include the Verizon Wireless Amphitheater and, when the Spurs aren't playing there, downtown's AT&T Center.

Latin American music and dancing is king in San Antonio's Southtown Arts and Entertainment District. Several clubs there swing to a Cuban, Argentinean, Mexican, or Brazilian beat. First Fridays of the month are the main event in Southtown, when shops, restaurants and clubs stay open late, and special arts events are held.

Hang out in San Antonio for any period of time, and you're likely to hear Conjunto and Tejano music.

Conjunto evolved at the end of the 19th century, when South Texas was swept by a wave of German immigrants who brought with them popular polkas and waltzes. These sounds were easily blended into Mexican folk music. Conjunto music often features the accordion and bajo sexto, a 12-string instrument used for rhythmic bass accompaniment.

Tejano (Spanish for "Texan") is a more modern version of conjunto. The accordion and the bajo sexton are prominent instruments in Tejano, but the music also draws from genres including pop, jazz and country. Conjunto and Tejano gained widespread recognition when Hispanic superstar Selena – who was well on her way to crossover success – was murdered in 1995.

Texas' largest single-day arts event, Luminaria, is held each March in San Antonio's historic downtown. The free showcase features all art forms including dance, literature, media, music, performance and visual arts. More than 315,000 people attended performances at eight stages during Luminaria 2013.

"This annual celebration of the arts has become a hallmark event, showcasing San Antonio as a creative and contemporary hub," San Antonio Mayor Julian Castro said in a news release about the festivities.

San Antonio's nurturing arts environment has yielded dozens of nationally known musicians over the years. A few of the most notable:

CHRISTOPHER CROSS

This singer-songwriter, born Christopher Charles Geppert, first played with a San Antonio-based cover band named Flash before signing a record deal with Warner Bros. He released his debut album, *Christopher Cross*, in 1979; it helped him make Grammy history by winning all four general Grammy awards (Record of the Year, Album of the Year, Song of the Year and Best New Artist) in the same year. That album also won a

Grammy for best musical arrangement for the single "Sailing." Among Cross' biggest hits are the songs "Ride Like the Wind," "Arthur's Theme" (which won the Oscar for Best Original Song in 1981) and "Think of Laura."

HOLLY DUNN

A country artist, Dunn first found fame with her 1986 Top-10 hit "Daddy's Hands." She had more than a dozen singles land on the country music charts, including two No. 1 hits: "Are You Ever Gonna Love Me" and "You Really Had Me Going." Dunn retired from music in 2003 and now works as a painter whose work is exhibited and sold in the southwestern United States.

EMILIO NAVAIRA

An American musician of Mexican descent, Emilio Navaira III (often referred to simply as "Emilio") performs both country and Tejano music. He has charted 10 singles on Billboard Hot Latin Tracks charts and six singles on the Billboard Hot Country Singles & Tracks charts. Emilio has been called the "Garth Brooks of Tejano." The San Antonio-based singer was awarded a 2008 Latin Grammy award for his album *De Nuevo*.

GEORGE STRAIT

This singer and music producer is often referred to as the "King of Country." He rocketed to success after his first single "Unwound" was a hit in 1981 and quickly became known for his unique blend of western swing and honky-tonk. Strait holds the world record for more No. 1 singles than any other artist in the history of music on any chart or in any genre, having recorded 59 number-one hit singles as of 2012. Strait has sold more than 70 million albums in the United States

Emilio Navaira

and his certifications from the RIAA include 13 multi-platinum, 33 platinum and 38 gold albums. In the 2000s, he was named Artist of the Decade by the Academy of Country Music and was elected into the Country Music Hall of Fame.

ERNEST TUBB

Nicknamed the "Texas Troubadour," Tubb was one of the pioneers of country music. His biggest career hit song, "Walking the Floor Over You," helped launch the honky tonk style of music. He recorded duets with the then up-and-coming Loretta Lynn in the early 1960s, including their hit "Sweet Thang." Tubb is a member of the Country Music Hall of Fame.

his mother realized that taking online classes at home would be a better option for him.

Austin's Internet fame didn't immediately translate to high-paying record deals and sold out arenas. At first, he played at parties – charging as much as $400 for a 45-minute set – and Skyped with fans for a fee. He sold his own merchandise and performed at PlayList Live, a convention featuring YouTube stars. In late 2012, a Chicago family paid Austin $2,000 to fly in and play at a party. After the performance, the teen singer announced – on very short notice – that he'd meet fans at Chicago's Millennium Park. In what Michelle refers to as a "watershed moment," nearly 1,000 Mahomies (the name he's given his fans) showed up and police had to be summoned to whisk Michelle and Austin away from the riotous crowd.

"That was a turning point," Michelle told *The Hollywood Reporter*, "when I

Austin visits the Empire State Building during a visit to New York City in late 2012.

After appearing on 'Live with Kelly and Michael' in September 2012, Austin took time for photos with fans.

MUSIC, FAME AND THE INTERNET

When Chad Hurley, Steve Chen and Jawed Karim founded YouTube in 2005, they envisioned it as a simple way to upload and share videos with friends. They hoped others would find the website useful, but they couldn't have imagined how incredibly popular it would become. Consider:

- As of April 2013, more than 1 billion unique users visit YouTube each month.
- More than 4 billion hours of video are watched each month on YouTube.
- 72 hours of video are uploaded to YouTube every minute.
- In 2011, YouTube had more than 1 trillion views – equal to approximately 140 views for every person on Earth.

The "discovery" of musician Austin Mahone can be attributed to viral YouTube videos of his performances – a story that's led critics and industry insiders to draw comparisons between him and Justin Bieber.

Austin and JB are definitely YouTube success stories, but they're hardly the first celebs to gain fame via online videos. A few others you may want to check out include:

PSY

Park Jae-Sang, the South Korean rapper better known as Psy, had released six albums before gaining international fame thanks to his catchy hit single "Gangnam Style."

Within the first nine months of its July 15, 2012, release on YouTube, "Gangnam Style" had been viewed more than 1.5 billion times. The song reached No. 1 on the iTunes sales chart and is the most viewed video in the history of YouTube. In 2012, Psy signed with Bieber's manager Scooter Braun and his Schoolboy Records.

ALEX DAY

Described as "one of Britain's most popular YouTubers," Alex Day created his first YouTube channel as a teenager, intent on producing a video podcast to entertain family and friends. He later produced a popular series of humorous videos entitled "Alex Reads *Twilight*," in which

he would read and critically analyze the popular young-adult novel *Twilight*; those videos have received 14 million views.

A talented musician, Day has since released two studio albums, two EPs and had three UK Top 40 hits. As of April 2013, his YouTube channel, nerimon, had nearly 700,000 subscribers; the official video for his single "Good Morning Sunshine" had been watched almost 1.7 million times.

ASHKON

Born to Iranian immigrants in Northern California, Ashkon is a rapper, singer/songwriter and actor. In 2006, Ashkon jumped onto the Bay Area hip-hop scene with his debut record *The Final Breakthrough*.

Two years later, he generated a great deal of buzz with his single "Hot Tubbin' (On the Late Night)." The video for the song became a viral sensation on YouTube, receiving approximately 700,000 views to date, thrusting Ashkon into the national spotlight. Ashkon had another huge Internet hit in 2010, when his San Francisco Giants-related "Don't Stop Believing" YouTube video became the official playoff anthem of the San Francisco Giants and to date has nearly 3 million views.

CHRISTINA GRIMMIE

Christina Grimmie was sitting in math class when she got an unusual text from her brother; he said Selena Gomez's stepfather was trying to contact her. Like thousands of other viewers, Brian Teefey saw her cover of Miley Cyrus' "Party in the U.S.A." on YouTube. It was only her second video on the site (the first was another Cyrus cover, "I Don't Wanna Be Torn"). But

believe it or not, becoming the next big thing wasn't her intention. She told ClevverTV: "It's shocking. I didn't go on YouTube for that. I went on YouTube just to see what would happen and then suddenly things blew up."

And she wasn't exaggerating. With more than 1.5 million subscribers, she became the fourth most subscribed musician on YouTube in May 2012 (as of May 2013, she's closing in on 2 million). She released her debut EP, *Find Me*, in 2011 along with the hit singles "Advice" and "Liar Liar." She's also toured with Selena Gomez, performed at the American Music Awards and has appeared on the *Ellen DeGeneres Show* and the Disney Channel's *So Random!*. She even started her own web series called *Power Up: with Christina Grimmie*.

Although she still doesn't know how she became so popular, Christina has some simple words of advice for anyone trying to be a YouTube star: be unique and ignore the haters.

Austin performs an acoustic song during Y100's Jingle Ball in Ft. Lauderdale, Fla., in December 2012.

started to realize that things were getting crazy."

In the fall of 2012, Austin's mom quit her job as a mortgage loan officer to focus on her son's career.

"We've been through a lot, and we've had a lot of faith that we'd get through it," Michelle said. "I always tell Austin not to take any of it for granted because the minute you do, it could be gone. We always talk about that – feeling blessed, because he is blessed."

Michelle read books and learned what she could about the music industry. Before long, though, she realized she needed help – things were simply happening too fast.

Michelle and Austin met with dozens of record label executives, producers, managers and songwriters before finally settling on the Miami-based management team at Chase Entertainment. In September 2012, Chase Records announced a deal with Universal Music to conduct distribution, marketing and radio promotions through Universal Republic. The first artist with an album release on the new imprint? None other than Austin!

A statement by Chase Records founders Rocco Valdes, Michael Blumstein and David Abram said: "We are so excited to join the Universal family. Their resources are second to none, their stable of artists is top notch, and their team of executives, A&R and radio reps are the strongest in the industry. We couldn't have asked for a better support system and are excited to have their resources and support to launch Chase Records and the career of teen phenom, Austin Mahone."

That Austin's star is rising doesn't seem to be much of a surprise to industry insiders.

Former American Idol judge Kara DioGuardi told *The Hollywood Reporter* that, in addition to musical talent, fans

Super, Secret Talent

Sure he can sing and dance and play the guitar, but Austin Mahone has talents you may not even know about.

"I can wiggle my ears," he told Scholastic's Stacks. And, as if that wasn't enough, he also has double-jointed thumbs. "I can pull (my thumb back). It looks like I broke it."

Now, *that's* talent.

are drawn to Austin because of his sincerity and openness. "He knows how to connect," she said. "I think people feel attached to him because he's so genuine. He lets (fans) into his bedroom and talks to them in his videos. He's got their notes on the wall ... It's very much what they're going through at that age. When you see him perform, it's like he's singing to you."

An authentic guy who's not putting on airs, who looks you in the eye when he talks to you, who's funny and cute and can sing – not Auto-tune singing, but real, from-the-heart singing? What's not to like about a guy like that? It appears music fans around the world are about to find out for themselves. ★

BREAKING ONTO THE MUSIC SCENE

You've got a decent voice, so why haven't you landed a record deal, become a recording artist and headlined your own cross-country concert tour? Why aren't you right there with Austin Mahone, ready to take on the music world?

Because it takes more than just good pipes to make it big.

Singer Joey McIntyre says no recording artist can be successful unless he or she breaks a few rules along the way.

"As a member of the New Kids on the Block, I helped sell 75 million records," he told the *Boston Herald*. "When I branched out as a solo artist, at first I had to finance my own efforts, because the record companies weren't telling me what I wanted to hear. There are so many levels of bureaucracy you have to navigate through in order to achieve any level of success in the recording industry."

Being at the top of your game is crucial and the way to get there is practice. Alicia Keys is a great example of an artist who made this rule work. She sang backup in numerous bands until she made her breakthrough with her Grammy Award-winning song "Fallin'."

"Music came before everything, everything, everything," Keys has said. "It just meant more than anything ever meant. I would risk everything for it."

Singing in the shower is great, but really practicing your craft takes more effort. Find a vocal coach, take a class, join a band, perform in an open mic night. Practice, practice, practice.

Whatever you do, don't give up. If you keep hearing "No," find out why. Do you need a hook that sets you apart from all the other acts trying to make it big? Do you need to change your look? Is your voice better suited to a different genre? Listen to feedback, weigh your options and be persistent.

"Often, what it takes to get your demo tape listened to comes down to who you know in the industry," says Denise George, National Director Pop Promotion at Jive Records. "This is a tough industry to succeed in," George said. "You have to really want to achieve success and be willing to dedicate your life to achieving it. Britney Spears, for example, has been performing since she was in preschool."

Photo courtesy of AP Images

New Kids on the Block Joey McIntyre, Danny Wood, Jordan Knight and Jonathan Knight attend a publicity event in April 2013.

Learn as much as you can about the recording industry. Read publications like *Billboard* and *Radio and Records*, so you can stay on top of music trends. Attend local shows and talk to performers between sets, many – especially those just starting out – will be willing to share tips and information.

Don't forget that many of today's hottest musicians – including Austin, Justin Bieber and Cody Simpson – were discovered thanks to the Internet. Once your sound is refined, start uploading videos. Don't know how? Ask a friend, take a class or follow online tutorials – it's really not that hard.

While it may not be any great surprise that young people use YouTube to find and/or listen to music, there's now research to back that up. According to a Nielsen Music 360 report released in August 2012, 64 percent of teens say they listen to music through YouTube. The Web's leading video-sharing site topped all other music sources cited by teens; 56 percent said they listen to music on the radio, 53 percent rely on iTunes and 50 percent listen to CDs.

No doubt, the Internet can serve as an amazing promotional tool to help new artists get discovered. Remember that you want your videos to go viral because people are amazed by your talent – not because they're laughing at your not-so-hot dance moves.

Practice, persist and get smart about the industry – your future stardom depends on it.

CHAPTER TWO
MAKING MUSIC

For some it's flowers or candy or a romantic dinner for two.

Austin Mahone, however, did something a little different on Valentine's Day 2012: he released his first single, "11:11," on iTunes. The song, a pop gem inspired by the mystical powers of the time 11:11, charted at No. 19 on the Billboard Heatseekers Songs chart. It was an auspicious beginning to a promising musical career.

Three months later, on June 5, 2012, Austin released a second single called "Say Somethin'." The video for that catchy guitar-pop track capitalizes on Austin's wholesome good looks and nearly perfect smile and tells the story of trying to connect with a high school crush. It's a scenario – and song – that resonated with fans. The single charted at No. 34 on the Billboard Pop Songs chart. Within eight months of its release, the song's

Austin and his crew perform at Y100's Pre-Show at Jingle Ball Village in Fort Lauderdale in December 2012.

AUSTIN'S BTR CONNECTION

Mahomies know that Austin Mahone is a fan of Big Time Rush, so it really shouldn't have come as much of a surprise when MTV News announced the entertainers were teaming up for a TV project.

Big Time Rush announced that Austin is one of a handful of stars who will appear on the final episode of season four of their self-titled Nickelodeon series. Actor and rapper Nick Cannon, American pop duo Karmin and singer/songwriter Alexa Vega also are slated to appear in the episode, billed as "Big Time Awards Show."

The show's storyline revolves around the fictitious Tween Choice Awards, where the boy band is nominated and booked to close the show. But, before the foursome can take the stage, they uncover an evil plot to brainwash everyone in the audience. Big Time Rush must take down the bad guys and make sure the show rolls on as scheduled.

Big Time Rush airs on Nickelodeon. The show's fourth season will follow the band as they record their third album and prepare for a world tour in a changing pop-music landscape.

Kendall Schmidt, James Maslow, Carlos Pena, Jr. and Logan Henderson of Big Time Rush in Hollywood in April 2013.

> *Still without a label and with only two singles on iTunes, Austin accomplished another remarkable feat in June 2012. He sold out the 2,000-seat Best Buy Theatre in New York City in just 30 minutes.*

music video had accumulated more than 18.5 million views, proving Austin is a true force to be reckoned with on the pop scene.

"That feels amazing to know that I've come such a long way. I am so blessed to have so many amazing fans around me that have helped me reach my dreams," he told *Broken Records* magazine.

Still without a label and with only two singles on iTunes, Austin accomplished another remarkable feat in June 2012. He sold out the 2,000-seat Best Buy

Theatre in New York City in just 30 minutes. Even Austin was astonished by news of the sell-out.

"I wasn't ready for that one," he told *J-14* magazine. "I was in IHOP and when my mom told me I was like, 'Wow, that's crazy!'"

That New York City show, combined with fans clamoring for more, led Austin to take his show on the road, with performances in cities including Philadelphia, Los Angeles and Chicago.

On Dec. 3, 2012, Austin released "Say You're Just a Friend." The single, released on iTunes via Chase Records, features Flo Rida on rap vocals. The tune's catchy melody and chorus were inspired by rapper Biz Markie's 1989 song "Just a Friend."

"The single's about basically having that one person that you like very much and you have a crush on them and you tell them that you like that person more than a friend and she's saying, 'Ah, no, I like you just as friends,'" Austin told Entertainmentwise.com in April 2013. "So, I think everybody can relate to that."

Austin had long been a fan of Flo Rida, who is known for hit songs including

DUET PARTNER: ALYSSA SHOUSE

Sweater-wearing Austin Mahone sings his heart out on his cover of "No Air" (Chris Brown and Jordin Sparks). His angst-filled vocals are strong and he's handsome as ever – but who in the world is his equally fretful duet partner?

Ah, it's none other than Alyssa Shouse.

Shouse has grown up singing in school talent shows and competitions around her hometown of Ellicott City, Md. In December 2008, she began posting videos of her performances – a combination of covers and original songs – on YouTube.

"I had a lot of favorite singers on YouTube and it really made me want to do it too," she said in a 2010 interview with the online publication *YHP*. "I wanted to do it because I loved singing for people, so on YouTube I could sing for as many people as I could get. It wasn't really a way to get found, it was just a way to showcase what I love doing."

Oh, but she did "get found."

American singer/songwriter/producer/actor Jason Derulo saw Shouse's videos online and signed her to his new label, Future History, in summer 2010.

From there, she recorded and released her first single, "Overnight Celebrity." She's performed around the country and made appearances on shows including MTV's *The Seven*. As of April 2013, her YouTube channel had

Jordin Sparks and Chris Brown made "No Air" famous, but Austin and Alyssa performed a pretty decent cover of the song.

attracted 137,400 subscribers and her videos had been viewed nearly 11 million times.

Shouse says working with Derulo is as much fun as it is work. "We joke around all the time. He makes me really comfortable and we have the best time hanging out," she told Just Jared Jr. in 2011.

Derulo continues to be impressed with his online discovery. "If I had to compare her to anyone, I would say Christina Aguilera," he says. "She has a big voice in a little body."

Austin posted his duet with Shouse on YouTube in April 2012; within its first year online, the video had attracted nearly 2.6 million views.

"Low," featuring T-Pain and "Right Round," featuring Ke$ha.

"I thought it would be cool to get him on my next single so my managers called him up and he said he would do it," Austin said. "It's amazing, like I said, I've always loved his music and it was just an honor to work with him."

The high-energy single, which is also about crushes and young love, premiered on MTV on Feb. 7, 2013. Within three months of its debut on YouTube, the video had more than 16 million views. A few weeks after the flashy video debuted, a more straight-forward, vocals and piano video of the song was posted on YouTube; by May 1, 2013, it had attracted more than 1 million views.

Austin went into full heart-throb mode with the spring 2013 release of his video "Heart in My Hand." He ditched his signature baseball cap for the video and instead wore all white attire, from his shirt and pants right down to his tennis shoes. He ditched the choreographed dance and instead sits at a piano, longingly glancing into the camera – all while sitting on a beach near Miami.

The piano-driven video, directed by Austin's good friend Dave Brytus, was

White House Invite

How does a young pop star know when he's "made it"?

For Austin Mahone, a sure sign was when he was invited to perform at the 135th annual White House Easter Egg Roll on April 1, 2013. The event attracts more than 30,000 people to the South Lawn of 1600 Pennsylvania Avenue for games, stories and the traditional egg roll.

In a news release announcing his invitation to the event, Austin said, "When I started making videos online, I would have never imagined I would end up performing as part of such a long lasting White House tradition."

posted on YouTube on March 17, 2013, with this simple caption: "This is a song I wrote the other day and I shot a little video to it ... Just wanted to show you guys ... What do you think!?!"

What do fans think? It's clear they love their dreamy, beach-strolling Austin. YouTube commenters effused:

"He looks amazing in alllll white. He's so hottt. Love U Austin. Mahomie Forever."

AWARD NOMINATIONS - ALREADY!

Austin Mahone has barely dipped his toes into the entertainment industry, but he's already making an Olympian-like splash.

For starters, Austin beat out Ryan Beatty, IM5, Cimbrelli and Christina Grimmie to be named Best Breakout Star at the 2013 Radio Disney Awards.

"Wow, I've never won an award before," he said while accepting his statuette. He went on to thank his fans and his mom, "This is amazing. First of all, I want to thank all the Mahomies out there."

He was nominated for four additional awards that night: Best Male Artist, Fiercest Fans, Best Crush Song and Best Acoustic Performance. Sure, Justin Bieber won Best Male Artist, but just being nominated alongside him, Cody Simpson and Bruno Mars made Mahone a pretty happy guy.

In early 2013, Austin was nominated for a Popdust/Popstar of Tomorrow award. He was edged out by Fifth Harmony, an American five-piece girl group that was formed for the second season of *The X Factor*.

And, while he may not have gotten a trophy to go with the title, Austin was named *J-14*'s Icon of Tomorrow in late 2012. The magazine recognized "iconic" figures in 26 categories including Iconic

Song, Iconic Trendsetter, Iconic Tweeter and Iconic Couple. The 2011 winners of the Icon of Tomorrow Award have gone on to some pretty big things ... you may have heard of them ... One Direction?

It's nearly certain that Austin's mantel will be filled with awards in no time at all ... let the nominations begin.

Austin proudly accepts his Golden Mickey Mouse statuette during the 2013 Radio Disney Music Awards in Los Angeles. Photo courtesy of AP Images

"More handsome than Bieber. Yeaay."

"I LUV that song. I heard it already like 500 times I just can't get enough plus he's so cute."

"Ahhhh, I found my new favorite song – I love u Austin."

"I listen to this every time I am sad or happy. P.S. – There's no one hotter than you Austin Mahone and you are my fav singer. You're better than Pink, JB, Drake and Hollywood Undead combined."

Within just two months of its release, the video for "Heart in My Hand" had attracted more than 2.8 million views – a sure sign that fans are clamoring for more.

Even as celebrity status sets in, Austin remains devoted to his music and his fans.

His days are jam-packed with radio interviews, TV appearances, magazine interviews and concerts. A May 2013 show in Mexico City offered proof that Austin's fame reaches far beyond the U.S. borders. Hundreds of Mahomies waited for him outside Universal Republic's Mexico City offices and they went absolutely gaga when they finally caught a glimpse of their idol. Members of the mostly female crowd screamed and squealed when Austin waved from a second floor window – some girls even climbed trees to get closer to the singer.

Undeterred by all the distractions, Austin is putting the finishing touches on his full-length debut album. The project, which will feature production from Bei Maejor, will be marketed and distributed by Chase/Universal Republic.

"I'm getting pressure from my fans and I'm still working on it, but the sound is going to be like 'Say Somethin' – happy, upbeat," Austin told *Bop/Tiger Beat*. "I'm also going to have some ballads on there, maybe a couple urban songs, more R&B. But it's basically going to be mostly like 'Say Somethin'."

Alright, say Mahomies, just bring it on. ★

Austin and T-Pain pose backstage at Power 96.1's Jingle Ball 2012 in December 2012 in Atlanta.

AUSTIN'S MUSICAL INFLUENCES

Artists develop their own sound based on the influences in their lives.

They often reinterpret music from their childhoods, add recycled rhythms from their teen years and create arrangements that are both inspired by the past, yet are still oh, so very original. Everyone does it.

• Michael Jackson said he was influenced by artists including Little Richard, James Brown and Diana Ross.

• Beyonce Knowles said Mariah Carey's singing influenced her to practice vocal runs as a child.

• Michael Jackson, Stevie Wonder, Usher and Justin Timberlake are among Justin Bieber's many musical influences.

Austin Mahone is no different. His music is made up of a little bit of everything.

"I grew up listening to country music because that was what my mom listened to at the time," he said in a March 2013 interview for VEVO LIFT. He enjoyed singing along to George Strait and the first concert he ever attended was headlined by country star Kenny Chesney.

As he matured and began branching out musically, Austin began to listen to other genres including R&B and pop. He became a fan of artists as diverse as rappers Flo Rida and Drake, R&B artist Ne-Yo, pop singer Justin Bieber, and country/pop artist Taylor Swift.

"I found an artist named T-Pain so I really attached to his music and loved it so much," he

> *"I think an awesome Mahone, T-Pain, Chris Brown song would be pretty cool," Austin said.*

said. "That's what really crossed me over from listening to country."

Singling out the performer whose style has been most influential to his career is difficult for Austin, but he finally settles on an answer – Chris Brown.

"An inspiration to me would have to be Chris Brown because he's an amazing singer, an amazing dancer, he's an awesome performer," he said, noting that his favorite Chris Brown song is "Don't Judge Me."

"(I like) the lyrics behind it and I also like how the song was made – you know, the production of it," he said.

Is a future collaboration with some of his musical idols a possibility? Austin certainly wouldn't rule it out.

"I think an awesome Mahone, T-Pain, Chris Brown song would be pretty cool," he said.

OPENING FOR TAYLOR SWIFT

When Austin Mahone got the call that he would be opening for selected shows of Taylor Swift's highly anticipated RED Tour, he was elated.

"I still can't believe I'm opening for Taylor! I'm so appreciative and excited for this opportunity," he told Artist Direct. "Getting to play in stadiums, and it's with one of the biggest artists in the world! I can't wait!"

Prior to the tour's kick off, Austin told Just Jared Jr. he was thrilled with the idea of being able to perform for such huge audiences; several of the stadium shows will have crowds of 70,000 or more.

"I've never performed for that big of a crowd before," he said. "I'm not really sure what to expect because I've never been on tour before, but I think it's going to be fun. I've been rehearsing for a while now, just getting ready for all the shows."

Austin admits he's long been a fan of Taylor Swift. He was actually starstruck when, in early 2012, he got to meet her in a Nashville café.

"She walked in and I went up to her and was like, 'Can I have a picture with you?' I got a picture of her and I told her that I'm on YouTube and I sing. She was like, 'That's really cool. Keep up the hard work. Never give up on your dreams.' It's crazy. Now a year later, I'm going on tour with her."

Austin took another photo of himself with Taylor a year later – this time backstage prior to their show in Detroit, Mich. He posted the picture on Instagram with the caption: "It's been a year, but we've finally re-united! Thanks again @TaylorSwift13 for having me on the tour!! #REDTOUR"

Austin's shows with Taylor Swift were scheduled throughout the spring and summer of 2013 and were not consecutive:

May 4	Ford Field, Detroit, Mich.
May 25	Dallas Cowboys Stadium, Arlington, Texas
June 14	Rogers Centre, Toronto, Canada
June 15	Rogers Centre, Toronto, Canada
June 22	Investors Group Field, Winnipeg, Canada
June 29	BC Place, Vancouver, Canada
July 6	Heinz Field, Pittsburgh, Penn.
July 13	MetLife Stadium, East Rutherford, N.J.
July 19	Lincoln Financial Field, Philadelphia, Penn.
July 20	Lincoln Financial Field, Philadelphia, Penn.
July 26	Gillette Stadium, Foxboro, Mass.
July 27	Gillette Stadium, Foxboro, Mass.
Aug. 10	Soldier Field, Chicago, Ill.

Austin, Taylor Swift and Ed Sheeran gather in Club Red prior to their May 4, 2013, show at Ford Field in Detroit; it was the first of 13 North American dates that Austin appeared as part of the RED Tour.

CHAPTER THREE
HEIR TO THE POP THRONE?

The comparisons were inevitable.

• Justin Bieber was discovered thanks to YouTube. Austin Mahone was discovered thanks to YouTube.

• Justin connects with fans via Twitter and Skype. Austin connects with fans via Twitter and Skype.

• Pop star Justin is known for his hair, his stylish sneakers and his dance moves. Pop star Austin is known for his hair, his stylish sneakers and his dance moves.

• JB was raised by a single mother. AM was raised by a single mother.

The Hollywood Reporter has referred to Austin as "Baby Bieber." *The Daily Mail* has called him the "New Justin Bieber." AOL.com has referred to the Texas native as "the second coming of Bieber." Yahoo News went so far as to ask: "Justin Bieber vs. Austin Mahone: Are They The Same Person?"

Even the *Wall Street Journal* got into the act when, in October 2012, columnist Marshall Heyman wrote: "Today's youth don't dream about playing center field for the Yankees or piloting a spacecraft to Mars. Instead, they aspire to become the next Bieber." Heyman's article went on to name Austin as one of the five leading contenders to be the next Justin Bieber.

Austin says the comparisons to Bieber are flattering and bring with them a certain amount of pressure. JB was, after all, named by *Forbes* as the third most powerful celeb in the world in 2012.

"I hope to be as successful as him someday, but I just want people to give me a chance, see me as my own artist and as Austin. That's all I ask," he told *Extra* in April 2013.

Austin's fans, however, are often annoyed by all the talk of Justin.

"People say that Austin is the new Justin Bieber – I don't think that at all," fan

The Making of Mahomies

Everybody knows that Austin Mahone's fans are Mahomies. It's a name he came up with himself.

"I was sitting in my room with my best friend and we were talking about all these crazy fan names that people have and so we were like, 'If we had a fan base one day what would we name them?' And I came up with Mahomies for mine and I guess I told someone and word kind of spread," he told *4 Music*.

Austin and Justin Bieber strike a pose while visiting the Elvis Duran Z100 Morning Show in New York City in June 2012.

AUSTIN VS. JUSTIN

How about a side-by-side comparison of these two totally ahhhh-some performers?

	AUSTIN	JUSTIN
Middle name	Carter	Drew
Rightie or leftie?	Rightie	Leftie
Eye color	Hazel	Brown
Instruments	Piano, guitar, drums	Trumpet, guitar, piano, drums
Fans called	Mahomies	Beliebers
Sport of choice	Basketball, football	Ice hockey
Favorite team	San Antonio Spurs	Cleveland Cavaliers, Toronto Maple Leafs
Astrological sign	Aries	Pisces
National anthem	*Star Spangled Banner*	*O Canada*
Twitter followers	2.7 million	39.4 million
Favorite color	Red	Purple
Musical influences	Drake, Justin Bieber, Ne-Yo	Michael Jackson, Usher
Favorite foods	Pizza, Ziti, Lasagna, Chicken Alfredo	Spaghetti Bolognese
Favorite ice cream flavor	Vanilla, Chocolate	Cotton Candy
Favorite candy	Hershey's Kisses	Marshmallow Peeps
Personal motto	"Make the most of every opportunity, because you only get one chance."	"Family first."

AUSTIN

JUSTIN

Austin attends the 7th Annual J-14 magazine InTune Concert in New York City in September 2012.

Maggie Benzenhafer told MTV News as she waited outside his show at New York's Best Buy Theatre in June 2012. "I think Austin's going to be the new Austin Mahone."

That Austin's accomplishments are being compared to Bieber's shouldn't really surprise – or irritate anyone. After all, comparisons like this have been going on for years.

Lady Gaga has been hailed as "the new Madonna."

Bruno Mars has been called "the reincarnation of Michael Jackson."

The band fun. has been described as "this generation's Queen."

Jennifer Hudson has been described as "the new Whitney Houston."

Most of these assessments come about quite naturally. You hear a song

Austin doesn't mind comparisons to Justin Bieber – they are both great singers and dancers – but he'd like to be judged on his own merits.

IT'S ALL ABOUT THE HAIR

Yes, Austin Mahone's smile is adorable and his vocals are velvety, but everybody knows pop stardom is about having the right hair. Good news – Austin's locks are tops.

In September 2012, Austin got a trim and tweeted a photo of his new, shorter 'do along with the caption: "What do you think? New hairstyle? :)"

MTV's Buzzworth Blog writers immediately responded: "We really appreciate that Austin

asked us for our opinion, and we're gonna be completely honest about the way we feel: WE. ADORE. IT! Not only is the hair-to-gel ratio absolutely perfect (dudes, crunchy hair is just NOT OK – capiche?!)"

It wasn't the first time Austin sent his fans into a hair-induced frenzy – and it won't be the last.

On June 6, 2012, Austin tweeted a Photoshopped picture of himself with poorly dyed golden locks, accompanied by the message: "What do you guys think of my new dyed hair? (: "

Later the same day, he sent out photographic proof that his brunette hair was still very brunette along with this message: "Hahaha I'm just playin! (; I would never dye my hair that drastic!"

On March 29, 2013, Austin tweeted to fans that he was going to get a haircut. A follow-up tweet read: "AHHHHH she messed up my hair!!! WE HAD TO SHAVE IT!!" He eventually revealed that he was only joking and sent out a photo of his new hairstyle (which looked a lot like an old Justin Bieber hairstyle).

With all this fuss about follicles, it's interesting to note that Austin wears a hat almost everywhere he goes.

"The reason behind that is because I hate the way my hair looks," he told Just Jared Jr. in February 2013, "so I wear a hat to cover it up."

Girls love Austin's locks, but he'd prefer to hide them under a hat.

by a new artist, you try to describe that artist's style and sound to a friend and, in doing so, you rely on descriptions of music your friend already knows, such as "She sounds a little like Adele." Your friend knows exactly what Adele sounds like, so she can begin to imagine this new artist's contralto. Similar comparisons can be made for appearance, style or background. Before you know it, the media is suggesting the same sort of similarities.

These evaluations and labels don't suggest an artist is an imitator (though many openly admit to having shaped their style on the riffs of those who came before them). Instead, they often make the "new" artist more relatable for music fans and actually encourage people to sample music they might otherwise never hear.

Yes, Austin does admire the success Bieber has enjoyed. Yes, he understands that they were discovered in similar ways and attract the same sort of young, mostly female audiences. Still, he promises he won't be emulating any of JB's most recent bad boy behavior. A few of Bieber's headline-grabbing discretions?

- Disrobing in a Polish airport.
- Having his monkey seized by customs officials in Germany.
- Scuffling with the paparazzi.

The Globe and Mail, a newspaper published in his native Canada, has labeled Bieber "a national embarrassment." *Forbes* magazine has referred to him as a "spoiled brat" and the *Business Insider* has run articles about his "downward spiral."

Austin says seeing the negative attention heaped on Bieber has made him more determined than ever to stay on the straight-and-narrow.

What About Alex?

Austin Mahone famously posted those first YouTube videos with his best bud, Alex Constancio. What happened to Alex when Austin got famous?

Good news, the guys are still best friends. Alex doesn't sing much (though he does enjoy lip synching). He often travels with Austin, acts (he was in Rebecca Black's "Person of Interest" video), has his own merchandise line, and he's amassed nearly 335,000 followers on Twitter.

HE'S FASHIONABLE —FROM HEAD TO TOE

Austin Mahone is a fashion trendsetter. The handsome brunette is known for wearing baseball caps – typically backward. And, like any self-respecting pop star, he loves his outrageously stylish tennis shoes.

"I think I have more hats only because I have a hat for pretty much every day of the year," he told radio interviewer Mike Adam in early 2013. "I mean, I've always loved hats and sneakers, but once I started getting more into the music and doing a lot more photo shoots, they just sort of started flooding in."

Even still, Austin's shoe collection is impressive – so impressive, in fact, that VEVO

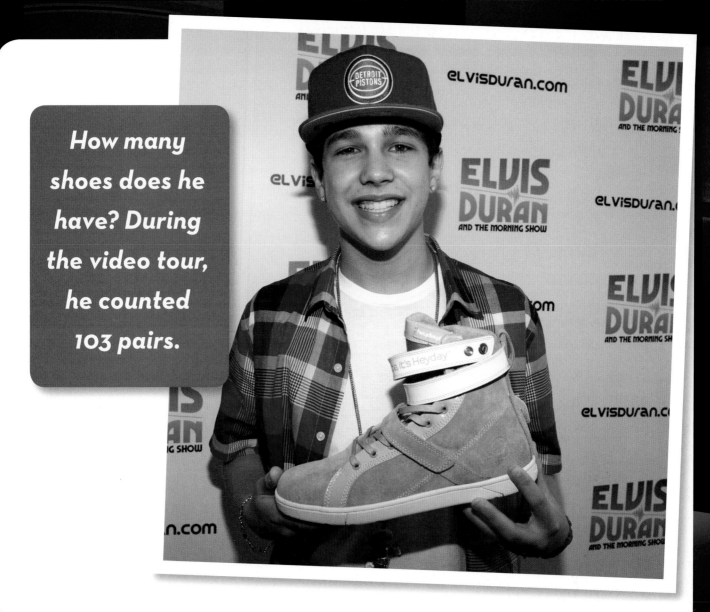

How many shoes does he have? During the video tour, he counted 103 pairs.

LIFT posted a video tour of his closet in March 2013. The three-minute segment has been viewed more than 350,000 times.

During the tour, Austin shows off the first sneakers from his extensive collection: a pair of white and red Nike Dunks. He then points to a spot in his impeccable closet (does it always look that neat?) where he keeps his favorite shoes. Among his top picks? A pair of all-red Puma high tops, some white Adidas, blue Nike Dunks and a pair of tan Timberland hiking boots that "go with anything."

Sure, most of the shoes are purely for fashion and he loves color coordinating with outfits, but Austin says some shoes actually help him dance better.

Austin admits that Nike and Adidas are his favorite brands, but adds, "If I see a pair of shoes that I like, then I'll just snatch them up."

How many shoes does he have? During the video tour, he counted 103 pairs.

"I was hoping I would break 100, so I think I met my goal," he said, noting that he's had as many as 105 pairs – but he lost two in a basketball bet with friends.

All a-Twitter

Austin Mahone loves online social networking. He especially loves connecting with his fans through Twitter. As of May 2013, he had 2.7 million Twitter followers and was gaining new followers at a rate of 6,820 per day.

Austin's tweets are rarely earth-shattering. Rather, he tends to update fans about what he's doing or where he is; he might tell a joke or make a random observation. On average, Austin tweets eight times each day. Some samples:

May 9, 2013: Dance rehearsals!!!

May 6, 2013: I need a button on my phone that will let me erase messages on other peoples phones that I've sent and regret very shortly after. lol

April 30, 2013: It's so funny trying to talk to people with the little Spanish I know!

April 26, 2013: I CAN'T WAIT FOR THE RADIO DISNEY AWARDS TOMORROW!!! #firstperformer

"I definitely have my family and my friends to keep me grounded and stay humble and I just gotta enjoy everything while I'm here and just enjoy life. It

might not be there forever," he told EntertainmentWise.

For those who are wondering, Austin did get a chance to meet Mr. Bieber in early 2012 (prior to most of JB's most notorious foul-ups) when the two entertainers were being interviewed at the same radio station.

"I was in the elevator and I went up to the floor and I got out of the elevator and he was standing right there, just like chilling. I said 'What's up Justin?' and I gave him a high-five and then he went to his interview. I went to mine and then we got some pictures and it was cool."

That first encounter didn't give the two pop stars much time to chat, but the Biebs was kind enough to offer Austin advice over the radio.

"He said that no matter how big or successful I get, not to stop and be like 'Oh, I'm here,'" Austin recounted for *Access Hollywood*. "He said to keep going and do different things and to keep pushing and just keep going to the top."

The top? Yes, that's exactly where Austin is headed. ★

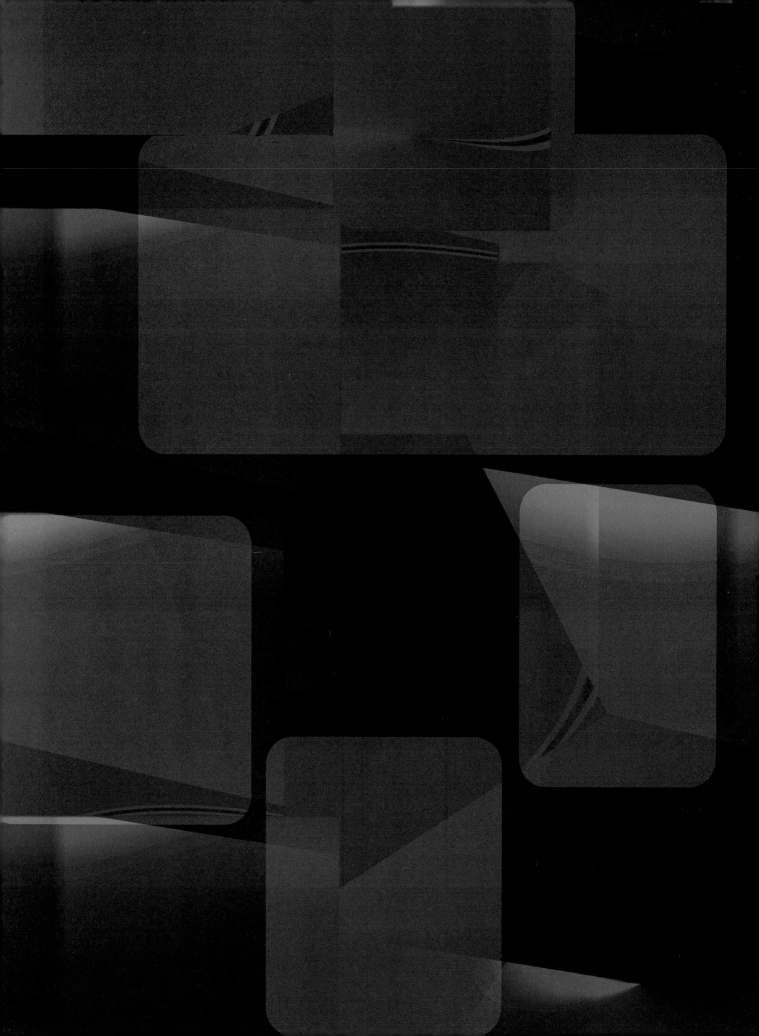

CHAPTER FOUR
ARE YOU A MAHOMIE?

New Jersey teen Ashley Filipe got to see Austin Mahone perform at New York's Highline Ballroom in March 13, as part of MTV's Artists to Watch showcase. The sold-out crowd chanted his name and sang along to his hit single "Say Somethin'," while Austin reached out to greet fans near the stage.

The whole scene made Filipe a little woozy – in a good way. "He touched my hand five times," she told *MTV News*. "I was going to pass out. To be honest, I was shaking."

Fellow concert-goer Megan McHale, had a similar, stomach-churning reaction when Austin grabbed her cell phone during his performance and snapped a selfie.

"I want to throw up, I'm so excited," McHale screamed. "I'm speechless."

It seems Austin Mahone has the kind of star power that makes girls' stomachs churn and knees go weak. That dazzling smile, that beautiful, thick hair, those

> *The sold-out crowd chanted his name and sang along to his hit single "Say Somethin'," while Austin reached out to greet fans near the stage.*

high-energy dance moves – AM's got the stuff that has fans blogging and vlogging and Tweeting at breakneck speed. The really great part is that he knows he wouldn't be where he is at now without those fans, so he remains devoted to interacting with them.

Austin, after all, got his start posting videos on YouTube. Positive feedback encouraged him to post more videos. He blogged. He tweeted. He video chatted with fans. Austin says all that direct interaction has both propelled his career and helped him develop a strong relationship with his fans. He's offered video tours of his closet and bedroom (which is decorated with posters made by his fans). He's uploaded videotaped pool matches with his mother and basketball games with his pals. And, he's shared videos of his first driving lessons.

Austin blows kisses to the crowd during a December 2012 show in Atlanta.

ALL A-TWITTER

Austin Mahone loves to stay connected with his fans and one of his favorite ways to do that is through Twitter. As of May 2013, the Texas native had more than 2.7 million followers and was gaining new Twitter followers at a rate of almost 6,500 per day.

Using 140 characters or less, Austin lets fans know what he's doing, where he's at, what he's eating, what he's thinking and so on. Fans love it and frequently re-tweet Austin's messages – spreading the word about his music, award nominations and TV appearances. Of course, Twitter is a two-way street; Austin follows nearly 20,000 people, many of them fans.

Here's a sampling of some of Austin's micro-blogging:

@AustinMahone: The best feeling is when I look over at you and you are already looking at me. *May 12, 2013*

@AustinMahone: Happy Mother's Day to the #1 Mom in the world! @MicheleMahone U mean everything to me – I love you with all my heart. Hope ur day is amazing. *May 12, 2013*

@AustinMahone: It's funny how you can do nice things for people all the time and they never notice, but once you make one mistake it's never forgotten. *May 9, 2013*

@AustinMahone: The best kind of kiss is when you have to stop because you can't help but smile. *May 8, 2013*

@AustinMahone: Mom's spaghetti hits the spot! *May 8, 2013*

@AustinMahone: I need a button on my phone that will let me erase messages on other people's phones that I've sent and regret very shortly after. lol. *May 6, 2013*

@AustinMahone: WHAT AN AMAZING FIRST SHOW!!! :D Thank u again @TaylorSwift13 #REDTOUR. *May 4, 2013*

@AustinMahone: Just got a nice warm welcome at the airport from the Mexican Mahomies! *April 29, 2013*

@AustinMahone: My room feels like Antarctica!! *April 25, 2013*

@AustinMahone: I think I'm gonna go to Walmart and buy a 6-pack of Crush! haha it's still weird to me that my face is on a can of soda! *April 23, 2013*

@AustinMahone: They told me I wouldn't shine, that my dreams were stones of gray. But look at me now, living life. *April 19, 2013*

@AustinMahone: Watching the hunger games... "Welcome to the 74th annual Hunger Games!" Me: Ohhhhhh my gaaawd! How. Does. This. Happen. *April 14, 2013*

@AustinMahone: I am quite certain that with a nice guitar and a recording contract, I could save the world. *April 11, 2013*

@AustinMahone: BEST BIRTHDAY EVER! Thank you guys so much for your awesome tweets and birthday videos! – I LOVE YOU SO MUCH!!!!! *April 4, 2013*

@AustinMahone: Ballin at the White House on Obama's court! #EasterEggRoll @AttheWH. *March 31, 2013*

@AustinMahone: Be yourself. Be proud of who you are, and don't let anyone change that. We're all freaks. No one on earth is the same. *March 27, 2013*

"I try to keep it as real as possible," Austin told Fuse TV, "so they can see me how I am, in my environment, in my room, stuff like that."

Even while he was doing his own marketing and scheduling, Austin was surprised by his own fame when, in October 2011, he tweeted to fans in Chicago that he was planning a simple meet-and-greet in Millennium Park. Thousands of Mahomies rushed to the area causing quite an influx of excited and hyperventilating tweens and teens. Police whisked Austin and his mother away to a secure building next to the park until they could figure out what to do. Austin eventually took to Twitter to let fans know the event had been cancelled: *Mahomies, it's really hard for me to say this but i can't do a meetup on*

Backup Plan

If music doesn't work out, Austin Mahone has another career path he wouldn't mind following – basketball. He used to play point guard when he was in school.

Famous Fan

One of Austin Mahone's most famous fans also happens to be Justin Bieber's ex Selena Gomez. Call it Lone Star love, Gomez grew up in Grand Prairie Texas, about 250 miles from Austin's hometown of San Antonio.

this trip – the police won't let me do it, I'm so sorry ... Don't worry I'm okay and you didn't do anything wrong!!

"It was really weird because I didn't have any security with me – it was just me and my mom – and I thought I was going to go and meet like 10 girls and I went there and it was like 1,000 girls and the police shut the whole thing down," he told *Access Hollywood*. "It was just crazy, just girls coming from all directions at me. It was just a whole new experience for me – coming from a super small town doing nothing and going to Chicago and getting destroyed by girls."

That fanatic fan gathering signaled to Austin that he needed a management team and he needed security. Both have since been put in place and subsequent fan encounters have been substantially less frightening.

HOW TO BE A FANTASTIC FAN

Some musicians' fans are just plain rude. Austin Mahone is proud to say his fans are a pretty respectful – and energetic – group. Anyone can say they're a Mahomie, but adhering to these five guidelines will ensure Austin's fans remain the best in the business:

1. Know Your Stuff. Read magazine and newspaper interviews, watch Austin's TV appearances, follow him on Twitter and, of course, listen to his music. Get your Austin info from a variety of sources so you can promptly spot misinformation.

2. Don't Stalk. Speak positively about Austin, support him and his music, but also remember to respect his privacy – that also goes for his family, friends and girlfriends. R-E-S-P-E-C-T.

3. Don't Dis. While we're talking about respect, we might as well mention respecting other artists, fans and fandoms. You've chosen to support an artist you deem worthy of your time and attention; others have chosen to support other musicians that suit their own tastes and preferences. Austin is a terrific musician – but he's not the only musician. Don't dis non-Mahomies.

4. Be Reasonable. It's okay to tell a friend why you don't care for another celebrity, but do it without getting too personal. No bashing and no bullying. Don't sabotage other celebrities' appearances or other fandoms' votes or meetings. Disruption is not reasonable.

5. Don't Go Crazy. Yes, it's understandable that you'd be excited if you got a chance to meet Austin – but imagine the noise and stress to which he's constantly being exposed. Showing your love doesn't have to mean screaming nonstop during a 30-minute set. And, no matter the circumstances: safety comes first. Don't push, don't climb fences or open doors you don't have permission to open, don't break traffic rules. Be smart!

Photo courtesy of AP Images

I came 2 C U ♥ AUSTIN

With throngs of fans growing, Austin still graciously stops for photos, to shake hands and, when it's possible, to autograph memorabilia. He continues his Twitter conversations with Mahomies; in addition to his 2.7 million followers, he follows more than 20,000 people – many of them his own fans.

And, the young Texas native is coming to grips with the fact that his fame has reached beyond U.S. borders.

Even before his debut album was released, Austin had amassed a legion of fans from around the world. He made stops in England in late 2012 and in Germany in early 2013. Meanwhile, fans in countries ranging from Japan and Australia to Scotland and Costa Rica had begun petitions aimed at getting Austin to perform there.

In May 2013, Austin was swarmed by fans when he traveled to Mexico City.

Austin answers questions for Canadian fans during an interview at MuchMusic Headquarters in Toronto in December 2012.

Hundreds of Mahomies waited for him outside Universal Republic offices and they went absolutely berserk when they finally caught a glimpse of their idol. Video clips posted by Austin's record company showed the largely female crowd screaming uncontrollably when the pop star appeared at a second floor window. The girls jumped, screamed, chanted and even climbed trees to get a better view of the singer. For his part, a sombrero-wearing Austin giggled, waved and videotaped some of the madness on his cell phone.

Longtime fans are realistic. Sure, they were cheering him on when no one else even knew his name, but they understand that Austin's increasing fame will put more demands on his time and attention. Video chats from his bedroom aren't likely to be as commonplace. Catching his attention at a stadium concert won't be as easy as it was at a free mall show a couple of years ago. Things change; for Austin those changes have been massive.

During a March 2013 live chat, fans repeatedly Tweeted their love to Austin. Then, this message popped up:

@ObeyMahoneee: *I hope you still* **interact** *with your* **fans** *when you hit like 10 million followers.*

Austin was quick to respond in the exact way fans hoped he would:

@AustinMahone: *you know i will! (: ★*

Three Fun Facts

Think you know everything there is to know about Austin Mahone?

Did you know:

1. He considers himself a paranoid person.
2. He hates slow drivers.
3. He's obsessed with pizza and eats it nearly every day.

Are You Austin's Dream Girl?

Sincerity. That's what Austin Mahone told *Popstar* magazine he looks for in a potential girlfriend. First date turn-offs? "No manners, on her phone."

"I like a girl who wants me for who I am," Austin said in a video interview for a fan site. "I like a nice smile and nice eyes."

AM APPAREL AND MORE

Dreaming of having Austin Mahone wrap his arms around you? We can't guarantee that's going to happen, but thanks to a wide array of available AM apparel, you can now snuggle up inside an Austin hoody.

Austin-inspired merchandise is available at his appearances and via his official website: www.austinmahone.com.

You can decorate your room with an Austin Mahone poster or pillow. Or, you can take the handsome singer to school with you in the form of an Austin bookmark or pen.

Of course, Austin's image is also emblazoned across T-shirts in more than 20 different designs and colors. There are also bracelets and hooded sweatshirts, both emblazoned with Austin's motto: "Haters gonna hate, Mahomies gonna love."

As Austin's fame grows so do his merchandising possibilities. Judging by those who've gone before him, there's no limit to the types of items on which his image might be printed. Some of the most outlandish fan merchandise out there? We're glad you asked:

• Detroit techno producer Omar S sells his own Omar S branded ice cube trays. What fan wouldn't want to be reminded of his favorite artist every time he wants a cold beverage?

• Love Justin Bieber? You can celebrate your birthday with a very unofficial JB piñata available through online party suppliers.

• The alternative rock band Weezer proudly sells Weezer-branded Snuggies via its website. Known as "Wuggies," the $30 blankets with sleeves, are available in three colors as well as a zebra-inspired print.

• In support of its single "Broken, Beat, & Scarred," heavy metal band Metallica offered up a collectible bandage tin. The $10 package, complete with band logo, contains 25 black adhesive bandages featuring the band's logo in red.

• The rock band KISS, long known for its face paint and flamboyant costumes, has had more than its share of unusual merchandise over the year. There have been caskets and cremation urns, Pez dispensers and biking shorts. Now, there are Kiss branded Mr. Potato Head dolls. The four figurines, which look like Kiss in spud form, cost $65.

Austin signs autographs as he arrives at Nickelodeon's 26th Annual Kids' Choice Awards in March 2013.

HOT SINGERS, HOT LYRICS

You love music. You love guys. And you love today's hottest male musicians. But are you really listening to the words they're singing?

Here's the test: Match these hunky singers to their lyrics. Answers are at the bottom of the page.

PITBULL

ADAM

JASON

1. **Cody Simpson**

2. **Usher**

3. **Jason Derulo**

4. **Taio Cruz**

5. **Chris Brown**

6. **Adam Levine**

7. **Austin Mahone**

8. **Pitbull**

9. **Drake**

10. **David Guetta**

11. **Bruno Mars**

12. **Justin Bieber**

A. "You know a lot of girls be...thinking my songs about them, this is not to get confused, this one's for you."

B. "Body rock, girl, I can feel your body rock. Take a bow, you're on the hottest ticket now."

C. "I want to be best. I want to be worst. I want to be the gravity in your universe."

D. "Burnin' up, burnin' up. Show 'em what you got."

E. "So dance, dance like it's the last, last night of your life, life."

F. "It's a beautiful night. We're looking for something dumb to do."

G. "I came to dance, dance, dance, dance."

H. "This melody was meant for you, just sing along to my stereo."

I. "I'm feeling like a star, you can't stop my shine. I'm lovin' cloud nine, my head's in the sky."

J. "You changed my whole life. Don't know what you're doing to me with your love."

K. "One, two, three, four. Uno, dos, tres, cuatro."

L. "I'm bulletproof, nothing to lose. Fire away, fire away. Ricochet, you take your aim."

Answers

1-C; 2-E; 3-I; 4-G; 5-J; 6-F; 7-H; 8-K; 9-A; 10-L; 11-F; 12-B

USHER

BRUNO

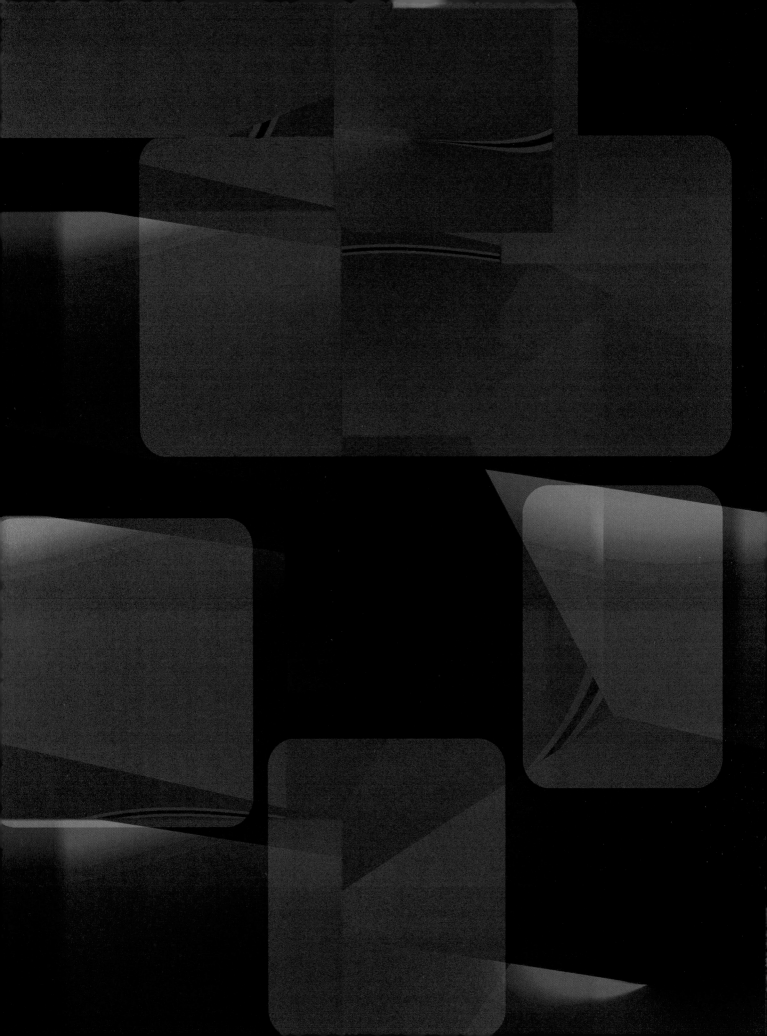

CHAPTER FIVE
WHAT DOES THE FUTURE HOLD?

Austin Mahone has been touring the United States and Europe, selling out smaller venues and opening stadium shows for one of the biggest stars on the planet. He's fully devoted to his craft and he has been doing hundreds of radio shows and television appearances nationwide. He's got his own management company and a record deal estimated to be worth $3 million to $4 million.

Yes, Austin is on top of the world.

Or, he will be when his debut album is finally released in Fall 2013. He's already released a string of catchy, danceable pop songs, but the album – originally slated for a April 2013 drop date – has been a little slow to come together. Austin's manager Rocco Valdes says that's because pinpointing Austin's sound took longer than anticipated.

"We were getting tracks in from so many great writers and producers and it was all over the place," Valdes told *Details* magazine, mentioning established hit-makers including Max Martin (Ace of Base, Backstreet Boys, Britney Spears), RedOne (Lady Gaga, Jennifer Lopez), Steve Mac (One Direction, Kelly Clarkson, Westlife), and Savan Kotecha (Britney Spears, One Direction). "I think Austin's lane is pop. I want this album to sound like the pop I grew up on – 'N Sync, Backstreet Boys, Britney – only updated."

RedOne, who produced the Lady Gaga hits "Just Dance" and "Poker Face," has been brought in to executive produce the album and provide big-picture guidance.

"It's been a little challenging," Austin told *Details*, "but I know my fans are gonna love it."

> **He's got his own management company and a record deal estimated to be worth $3 million to $4 million.**
>
> **Yes, Austin is on top of the world.**

Austin poses backstage during a December 2012 show in Atlanta.

While he waits for that album to come out, Austin continues to do what he does best – entertain and interact. He's excited about the prospect of promoting the album around the world.

"I can't wait to meet my fans in other countries," he told the website Musichel in March 2013.

Of course, Austin knows that celebrity often comes with its detractors – sometimes in the form of paid music critics. He knows their opinions matter because they generally broadcast their thoughts to a broad audience via newspaper, magazine, radio or Internet. And he's realistic enough to understand not every critic is going to love every song.

That said, early reviews of Austin's recordings and performances have been mostly positive. A sampling:

"(Austin) Mahone delivered an impressive performance complete with choreographed dances with his backup dancers. His finale of his new single, 'Say You're Just a Friend,' was met with more screams from the adoring teens and even some parents."

—Kelsey Auman in the *Buffalo (N.Y.) News*, writing about a December 2012 show at HSBC Arena

Give That Man a Burger

On more than one occasion, Austin Mahone has given a shout out to his favorite burger chain: Whataburger. It's a reference that's left many of his fans wondering what he's talking about. Whataburger was started in 1950 in Corpus Christi, Texas, by Harmon Dobson – a man determined to serve a burger so big that it took two hands to hold, and so good that after a single bite customers couldn't help but exclaim, "What a burger!" There are now 200 Whataburgers located across the southern United States.

"Austin Mahone is about to straight up conquer pop music. That takeover has been well underway for a while, and his latest single 'Say You're Just a Friend' featuring Flo Rida proves to be the next massive stop forward to the top ... With a presence of his own, an arsenal of hits already, and a whole lot of swagger, pop just might have a new king on its hands."

—Rick Florino for ArtistDirect.com, in his December 2012 review of "Say You're Just a Friend"

ARE YOU FOLLOWING AUSTIN?

Austin Mahone is a Twitter master. As of mid-May 2013, he had amassed nearly 2.7 million followers on the social networking site. It's an impressive figure for sure, but Austin is by no means the tweetingest tweeter on the planet. Twitaholic.com tracks top Twitter users based on followers. According to that website's computations, which are updated daily, the world's top Twitter users as of May 22, 2013, are:

Austin's Twitter stature is nothing to be ashamed of. In fact, the young pop star's legion of followers ranks him No. 422 among the world's 200 million Twitter users. Austin has more followers than some fairly notable folks, including: former Vice President Al Gore (425th), NBA great Kobe Bryant (No. 437th), Pope Francis (458th), actor/comedian Jamie Foxx (517th) and actress/singer Jennifer Hudson (593rd).

1. Justin Bieber (justinbieber)
   39,444,187 followers
2. Lady Gaga (ladygaga)
   37,492,181 followers
3. Katy Perry (katyperry)
   36,728,044 followers
4. Barack Obama (BarackObama)
   31,721,747 followers
5. Rihanna (rihanna)
   29,654,824 followers
6. YouTube (YouTube)
   27,947,511 followers
7. Taylor Swift (taylorswift13)
   27,636,732 followers
8. Britney Spears (britneyspears)
   27,000,434 followers
9. Shakira (shakira)
   20,728,194 followers
10. Justin Timberlake (jtimberlake)
    20,340,781 followers

Austin with the current No. 1 Twitter user, Justin Bieber.

RED Tour mates Ed Sheeran, Taylor Swift and Austin Mahone pose backstage before their sold-out show at Ford Field in Detroit.

"(Austin) Mahone skipped the live band in favor of four male dancers and a DJ. His music ('Say Somethin',' 'Hey Shawty') is standard teen-pop fluff, and he's clearly modeled after Justin Bieber. But Mahone, 16, is a confident, capable and charming performer ... Mahone wasn't always on key, but it's almost impossible not to be swayed by his earnestness."

—Joey Guerra in the *Houston Chronicle*, writing about a March 2013 show at RodeoHouston

"Mahone did not disappoint, igniting deafening screams when he hit the

For Austin, sneakers are the perfect red carpet footwear. He wore these high-tops to the 2013 Billboard Music Awards.

Radio personality Elvis Duran and Austin attend the Y100 Jingle Ball in Fort Lauderdale in December 2012.

stage and opened with 'Say Somethin'.' Backed by four dancers, a DJ/MC and occasionally a couple of backup singers, he showed off a dance-oriented, hip-hop/pop sound. He's more confident than the guy on the YouTube videos, but he still showed humility."

—Hector Saldaña for MySanAntonio.com, writing about a March 2013 show at RodeoHouston

"...17-year-old Internet sensation Austin Mahone drew a rapturous response for his slick, Bieberlike pop. He's definitely one we'll be hearing more from – if we can hear him above those screams."

—Gary Graff in the *News-Herald*, writing about a May 2013 show at Ford Field in Detroit

While great reviews certainly don't hurt, Austin knows it's his fans who will truly propel his career forward. His may

Ab-propriate

Yes, Austin Mahone has been working out with a personal trainer, getting himself in shape for both stardom and dating. But his mom says those awesome abs need to stay under wraps – at least for now. In spring 2013, Austin posted a shirtless selfie to Instagram; within an hour the photo had 20,000 likes. Austin's mom, Michelle, made him take it down asap. "I get it," he told *Details* magazine. "My fans are, like, from 2 to 21. I definitely want to please the parents."

not have the largest fanbase, but it is an active one. When he posted a photo of himself and tour mate Taylor Swift on Instagram on May 4, 2013, Mahomies went wild. Within two weeks, the picture had elicited 218,000 "likes" and nearly 10,000 "comments." A few weeks later, on May 17, 2013, he took to Twitter to announce: "Ok....The day has finally come!!! I will be releasing the first single from my ALBUM!!!!!!!!!!!!!!!!!" Within five days, that message was retweeted more than 10,000 times.

"I love (my fans) so much and everything they do for me," the singer wrote on his blog. "They are truly the

Shower Time

Grab a towel and turn on the water! Austin Mahone admits he loves to sing in the shower (who doesn't?). One of his favorite freshen-up tunes is "Let Me Love You" by Mario.

FAME ISN'T ALWAYS COMFORTABLE

When fame comes quickly – as it has for Austin Mahone – it can be overwhelming. All of the sudden you can't just walk through the mall without being stampeded by fans; your time simply isn't your own anymore.

Fame really is the ultimate Catch-22. Singers and actors work tirelessly to achieve fame. Then, when they achieve it, they learn they don't really get to simply be singers and actors anymore. They are put on pedestals because of their achievements. Suddenly they're role models whose every move is being watched: where they go, what they wear, who they're with, what they say. They're scrutinized and criticized and analyzed.

Austin seems to be adjusting well, but when the lack of privacy starts to bother him, he doesn't need to look far for empathy and advice. Here's what a handful of other celebrities have to say about the downside of fame:

Country singer **Carrie Underwood** shot to stardom thanks to her appearance on "American Idol." Since winning the 2005 version of that TV talent show, Underwood has recorded dozens of hits and won six Grammy Awards. She says her road to fame has been a bumpy one.

"At the beginning of my career, I used to have panic attacks. People were touching me, screaming – it made me really nervous," she told *Marie Claire* in May 2013. "In public, I just get nervous. It's a physical reaction, feeling like the walls are closing in. The fans are great. It's not their fault. I don't ever want to come across as ungrateful. But on my end, it is hard for me to process. Because I am still just me."

Thanks to *Twilight*, **Taylor Lautner** quickly became an A-list celebrity and heartthrob. The young actor appreciates his fame, but notes there's a downside all his success.

"When I am traveling the world promoting the films, I say I am on vacation, but it's not really true, I guess," he told Hollywood.com in September 2011. "When I go to a beautiful city, I spend the whole time in a hotel room and then I am back on a plane to the next place."

Lautner said his busy work schedule no longer allows time for relaxation. He said, "If I'm not filming, I'm promoting … I hang out with my friends, family, and kind of just – I don't even know. It's like, when I am not filming, it seems like – I don't even know what I do."

One Direction is the biggest band on the planet, but the strain of fame has ignited countless predictions and rumors about the group splitting up. **Zayn Malik** told *Fabulous* magazine that of the five guys in 1D, he's struggled the most with fame. He said online abuse against his family and religion has been particularly difficult to take.

Austin can't just play tourist anymore. Even his December 2012 trip to the Empire State Building was documented by photographers. Photo courtesy of AP Images

"I love the fact that I'm in a band, but it's very hard because of the type of person I was before," he said. "I was very reserved and just did my own thing. I guess I've probably found it the most difficult out of the boys."

The Hunger Games star **Jennifer Lawrence** told *Vanity Fair* magazine that she has more in common with her on-screen alter-ego, Katniss, than it might seem at first glance.

Like her character, she had a rapid rise from obscurity to stardom. And, she says, she often misses her more private, pre-fame life.

"I call my mom sobbing all the time," she said. "But (I'm) dealing with the repercussions of no more anonymity. You lose privacy."

best and most dedicated fans I know. Haterz can't hurt you unless you let them. And I just have one last thing to say.... Haterz gonna hate, Mahomies gonna love."

Ah, Mahomie love, it's a formidable thing.

Austin presents DJ David Guetta with the award for Top EDM Artist during the 2013 Billboard Music Awards.

"As a marketer, I know how devoted and powerful the Mahomies are," Charlie Welk, executive vice president of Republic Records told *Details* magazine. "You can laugh at the Mahomies, but they're serious. They're snipers."

Austin just hopes he's worthy of his fans' ongoing devotion. You see, this pop star thing isn't a passing fad for him.

"In 15 years, I see myself travelling all across the world, putting out albums and still making music," he said in a February 2013 interview on YouTube's Austin Mahone channel.

Of course, Austin knows he'll have to evolve as an artist to stay current; what works with fans when he's a teen won't fly with older crowds.

"For me, I'd say I'm going to go in the direction of whatever the hottest music is at that time," he said about future recordings. "I don't want to go in one direction and stay there; 10 years from now, music's gonna change, it's always going to change. So, I want to keep up with the music."

Keeping up or evolving into his own unique, one-of-a-kind sound? Only time will tell what the future holds for Austin Mahone. ★

Austin and Kelly Rowland team up to present an award at the 2013 Billboard Music Awards in Las Vegas.